up liberty's skirt

the poet's experience in New York City

up liberty's skirt

Ain't Got No Press

Front Cover Photo, Design, and Layout ~ Rick Lupert
Back Cover and Author Photos ~ Shira Kline

Thank you Kline, Cohens, Masengs, Constantine, Frank, Giuliani, Car Service, Bartholdi, Eiffel, Pulitzer, Mama's Food Shop, Nuyorican, Mole Sauce, King Kong, Two Boots, Grand Central Station, and subway entertainers everywhere.

Thanks especially to Amélie Frank for originally publishing this on Cassowary Press in August of 2001.

(818) 904-1021

or

15522 Stagg Street
Van Nuys, CA 91406

or

Rick@PoetrySuperHighway.com

or

http://PoetrySuperHighway.com/

First CreatSpace Edition ~ June, 2008

ISBN: 978-0-9727555-4-2 $8.00

contents

foreword

It was time to visit the big city. Sure, the city I live in is bigger; but that's not important. New York *is* the BIG CITY...it's certainly taller than Los Angeles. Jumping off half of the things in Manhattan is a lot more impressive than jumping off all of the things in L.A.

There's a lot to be said for compacting everything onto an island. Feel free to say any of those things. I'm not going to say them for you. Opinions are expensive in these parts. Send me a dollar, and I'll tell you what I think. I like Islands.

Brooklyn is not an Island. There is fabulous Mexican food there. The kind of food you wouldn't find on an island. The kind of food I wouldn't expect to find east of Arizona. When Shira told me she was taking me to Mexican food in Brooklyn, I told her that I come from the LAND of Mexican Food and laughed heartily. She was right though...right to take me there. It was Mexican food. It was good Mexican food. I've never been to Arizona.

So meet my trip to New York City. What is it that someone said to me after publishing *Feeding Holy Cats*? I think it was something like "Oh you with your books about the places you've been." It's true. New York is a place, and I have been there, and this book is all poems that I wrote there, except for the last two which I wrote in New Jersey, and the first few which I wrote on the way there. But the rest of them in the middle...oh yes, those were written in New York City. I found nothing unusual about the size of gravity revealing fruit.

Frank Sinatra, I love you.

To Shira

I
start spreading the news

I

At six AM
When it's still dark
and the shuttle is twenty minutes late
and you're standing outside
        in the cold
You begin to think about driving
        to New York City
SO you'll be three days late
The car is warm

II

"What does that Chinese symbol
tattooed to the back of your neck mean"

I want to ask the young woman
seated on the shuttle in front of me

I can tell by her knee that she's tall
"Taller than you" she would answer

III

Although we have not spoken,
the one thing we have in common
is our hatred of the third passenger

He is a six AM cellphone talking,
airport shuttle rider.

I hear him say the words
"Thirty nine million"

I hate him

IV

The driver asks if we are going to Chicago
He hopes not because the airport is shut down

Eight inches of snow

He says with the wisdom of a taxi driver
"No one is going to Chicago"

In The Terminal

Everyone headed to New York City
is wearing a long coat
They must know something

Flying to New York City

The Captain expects a choppy ride
all the way across the country
and not in the good karate kind of way

Weather Report

You can see your breath
in forty degree New York City weather
unlike in Los Angeles
where it is sixty five
and what you see in the air
is not your breath

I Don't Die

I meet Tracy the flight attendant
awaiting ground transportation

Six hours in the air and
she would kill me for a cigarette

I don't have one so
life goes on

Grand Central Station

I

They weren't kidding

II

In Grand Central Station
there are two kinds of people
Ones with long coats
and me

III

A woman goes to the MTA info window
Asks where she can get a grilled cheese sandwich
He tells her

IV

So this is where they've been keeping all the people

V

Inside a bathroom stall
graffitied on the door
in thick black ink

"I am what I am"

To think the moment of clarity
which must have taken place here

"Aren't we all" I mutter
and flush

VI

In the bathroom again
peeing next to Chasidic Jew
Black hat, black beard, open fly

I turn to this stranger
Fellow peeing Jew Brother
"So, you think the Messiah's going to come soon?"

VII

I stop to photograph the Mitzvah Wagon
in front of Grand Central station
The Chasidic Jew inside wants me
to stay and do Jewish things
"Can't, we're catching a train," I tell him
"We're all catching a train" he says
"It's all one big train."

II
these vagabond shoes

Family Reunion

Lunch with long lost uncle and cousin
Carnegie Deli. Sandwiches so big
You need a ladder to eat them

Knitting Factory One Night

I'm the only man in the club
This is my kind of place
I think

Trying To Impress The Mostly Lesbian Crowd

"I can go for days without breeding"

Assal Hygiene

Disposable toilet seat liners
are not found as frequently
in East Coast bathrooms
as they are in the west
where there is a greater awareness
of what comes into contact
with our asses

These Vagabond Socks

My right sock
tired of city block after city block
tries to hide in the shoe
My heels cry REVOLUTION
Don't wake me 'til Jersey!

Fight On The Subway

There's a fight on the Subway
Car in front of mine
Can't see anything
But the yelling
Which, of course
I can't see either

People lean through open car doors
for a glimpse of who is hitting who
The train can't move with the doors blocked

No one complains
Carnage unites underground New York
Home means another meal with the wife
all night sirens and a sleepless night

Leave the doors open another minute
I think there's blood on the floor

A tooth

Shira Is a Genius

the way she keeps her Metro Card
in her back pocket for easy access
while I fumble through my wallet
at the subway turnstile
backing up the 79th street station
for minutes

"By the way" she yells
"They're called 'stations,' not 'exits'"

I'm left on the Upper West Side
with my California showing

III
visiting the masengs

The Avian Maseng

I visit Danny on the Upper West Side
Minutes into the apartment and he's lost in Chi
Chi, his son's bird

Chi Chi refuses to kiss or sing
Looks at me with one eye

I have always made birds nervous

Terry

is unhappy with the election results
talks about Civil War
I think she wants one
It's not just the results
It's the idea
The glint in her eye when someone mentions
the midwest seceding
She sends her son to school
with the state flag
and a bayonet
just in case

Jonathan The Poet

has lost his bread somewhere in the house
searches everywhere for a sign
      yeasty residue
      a few crumbs
      footprints
Terry tells him to get a haircut
No mother
first the bread
always the bread

Danny Says

Wouldn't it be nice
if the new Guggenheim
blew into the river
so it could float
from place to place
like a traveling exhibit
with a glass bottom
for the kids
and excellent views
of Jimmy Hoffa

34

Danny Describes Nathan Kobrinsky in New York City

"What's your name sir" asks the hostess
"Peter" answers Nathan

The Haircutting Masengs

All of Danny's family needs a haircut
I head to the Lower East Side
So they can make an evening of it

IV
liberty

Burn Brooklyn Burn

From the back of the Statue of Liberty
it looks like she's walking to Brooklyn
either to set it on fire
or because there's good Mexican food there

Up Liberty's Skirt

I'm looking up the skirt
of the Statue of Liberty
She was, after all
made in France

I'm So Sorry

If you think I'm going to write something
about the sexual implications
of being inside the Statue of Liberty
You're dead wrong

Mowing Liberty

I see a John Deere Mower on Liberty Island
I assume they use this
to shave the Statues legs

The Old World

At Ellis Island
New Yorkers are herded into ships
for transport back to the old country
People are changing their names back
re-adding the *skis* and *oviches*
Life will be hard there
but it's home

Doesn't Like Her Job

I ask the woman at the Ellis Island Café
if the pizza is good New York pizza
She says she doesn't know because
she's not from New York

As if New Jersey is a place
you can actually be from

French Fries and a Slice of Pizza in the Ellis Island Café

It's my last meal
before I head back
to Bialystock, Poland
It's were I come from.
Nineteen-oh-five
I think my grandmother
left the stove on

Lost Luggage

The baggage room
with misplaced immigrant possessions
One hundred years, the Wolinsky family
still without their precious forks and spoons

V
epilogue

Rebirth

New York City ends
when the train from Penn Station
takes me to New Jersey
where I was born
thirty two years ago
haven't been back since
So I'm born again
as the train emerges from the harbor
into the Garden State
Run down buildings and
smoke stacks fill the windows
Things haven't been the same
since I left

Territory

Look at you New Jersey
stealing the coast from Connecticut
like a North American West Bank
controversial territory, not so wide
All Hartford wants
is a day at the beach

about the author

The author pictured with his hand up Liberty's nose.

Rick Lupert has been involved in the Los Angeles poetry community since 1990. He served for two years as a co-director of the Valley Contemporary Poets, a twenty-three year old non-profit organization which produces a regular reading series and publications out of the San Fernando Valley. His poetry has appeared in numerous magazines and literary journals, including *The Los Angeles Times, Chiron Review, Zuzu's Petals, Caffeine Magazine, Blue Satellite* and others. He recently edited *A Poet's Haggadah: Passover through the Eyes of Poets* anthology and is the author of eleven books: *Paris: It's The Cheese, I Am My Own Orange County, Mowing Fargo, I'm a Jew. Are You?, Stolen Mummies, I'd Like to Bake Your Goods, A Man With No Teeth Serves Us Breakfast* (Ain't Got No Press), *Lizard King of the Laundromat, Brendan Constantine is My Kind of Town* (Inevitable Press), *Feeding Holy Cats* (Cassowary Press). He has hosted the long running Cobalt Café reading series in Canoga Park since 1994 and is regularly featured at venues throughout Southern California.

Rick created and maintains the Poetry Super Highway, a major internet resource for poets. (PoetrySuperHighway.com)

Currently Rick works as the music teacher and graphic and web designer for Temple Ahavat Shalom in Northridge, CA and for anyone who would like to help pay his mortgage.

Rick's Other Books

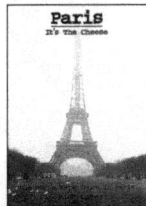

A Man With No Teeth Serves Us Breakfast
Ain't Got No Press
May, 2007

I'd Like to Bake Your Goods
Ain't Got No Press
January, 2006

STOLEN MUMMIES
Ain't Got No Press
February, 2003

BRENDAN CONSTANTINE IS MY KIND OF TOWN
Inevitable Press
September, 2001

FEEDING HOLY CATS
Cassowary Press
May, 2000

I'm a Jew, Are You?
Cassowary Press
May, 2000

MOWING FARGO
Sacred Beverage Press
December, 1998

Lizard King of the Laundromat
The Inevitable Press
February, 1998

I Am My Own Orange County
Ain't Got No Press
May, 1997

Paris: It's The Cheese
Ain't Got No Press
May, 1996

For more information:
http://PoetrySuperHighway.com/

www.ingramcontent.com/pod-product-compliance
Lightning Source LLC
Chambersburg PA
CBHW051048030426
42339CB00006B/243